Missing in Time

Missing in Time

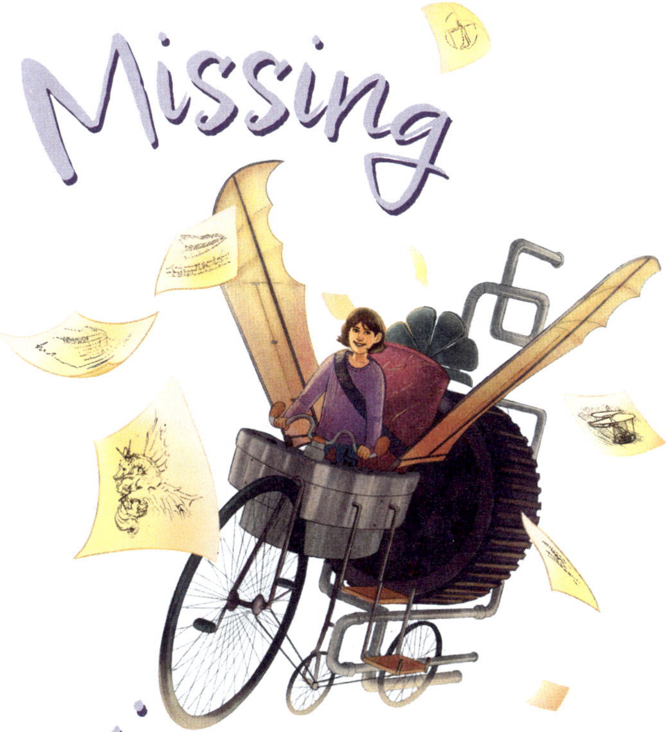

Liz Miles

Alisha Monnin

Collins

Contents

Chapter 1 Hidden in the basement 4

The time machine 14

Who was Leonardo da Vinci? 16

Chapter 2 Back in time. 18

Florence in the time of Leonardo da Vinci . . 30

Chapter 3 Leonardo da Vinci 32

Leonardo, the artist 44

Chapter 4 Good friends 46

Chapter 5 The experiment 58

The first aeroplane 68

Chapter 6 Lost and found 70

What Leonardo da Vinci left us 82

Renaissance women 84

About the author 86

About the illustrator. 88

Book chat. 90

MISSING!

Have you seen the explorer, Aldo Alberti?

Last seen in Florence, Italy

**Please contact: 81 Watchmakers Road,
Coventry**

My name is Maria, and this is my Great-Uncle Aldo. He disappeared ten years ago during a trip to Italy. I don't remember him because I was tiny then.

Mum says there was a MASSIVE search for him. Everyone was super worried. In the end, the police recorded him as missing. It was horribly sad. No one expected to see him again.

So my missing uncle is still a big mystery and I'm determined to solve it. One day, I'll find out what happened to him. Perhaps I'll even discover he's still alive.

Chapter 1 Hidden in the basement

Uncle Aldo lived in a small house in Coventry, the same city as me and my mum. He'd bought the house when he was a watchmaker, before he became an explorer!

After Aldo disappeared, his house became Mum's. That's because Mum was Aldo's niece and his closest relative. But Mum felt funny moving into his home, so she left it empty – hoping that Aldo would come back.

Then our rent went up, and Mum couldn't pay all the bills. So, one day, she said, "I hate to do this, Maria, but we'll have to sell Aldo's house. I feel sad about it, but I've got no choice."

I was sad, too, as it felt like we were giving up on him being found. I hugged Mum and said, "I'm sure Uncle Aldo would be pleased. He wouldn't want us struggling, would he?"

So the next weekend we set off to tidy the house, ready to sell. I desperately hoped I'd find some clue about what happened to Uncle Aldo.

The house was down a narrow, terraced street. It smelled musty and was full of dust. Mum opened all the windows and went upstairs to start sorting out Uncle Aldo's clothes for the charity shops.

I was sweeping the hall, when I spotted a rusty key hanging from a hook. I decided to explore.

The key opened a small door under the stairs. With a click and a shove, it swung open. There was a draught of icy, oily-smelling air. I pulled a string that hung from the ceiling and a faint orange bulb lit up the steps leading down to a basement.

I crept down the creaking wooden steps. Cobwebs brushed my cheek and the dust made me sneeze. At the bottom, a black curtain blocked the way. I pulled it aside and ... screamed!

Mum can't have heard me because she didn't come running. I stood, frozen to the spot, staring at a MASSIVE winged insect – it was so big it filled the whole room!

I started to tremble – what if it saw me? Slowly, my eyes got used to the dim light. The shape got clearer. It wasn't an insect at all! It was a machine made from bits of bicycle, cogs and wheels.
The "wings" were struts of metal, covered in canvas.

All around, prints of old drawings and paintings were taped to the walls. I recognised one from an art lesson – it was the *Mona Lisa*, a famous painting of a woman whose gaze follows you around. There was a strange picture of a star-shaped man, too. Above, in big loopy writing: *Leonardo da Vinci*. Then I spotted a note. I held my breath as I read …

> Whoever finds this – it was meant to be!
>
> I am Aldo, an explorer of time, and I'm on my grandest adventure. I have travelled back to my favourite time!
>
> I'm sending my machine back home so that someone else might use it. If you have courage, get on board and follow me!
>
> Two important things if you use my time machine (my very own invention!):
>
> 1) Don't worry: While you're away, time in the present will stand still. No one will notice that you've gone.
>
> 2) Beware: Do NOT forget this number. You will need it to get back: 8888.
>
> Use the machine wisely and keep it a secret.
>   Aldo

What? This can't be true. Time machines are made-up things in stories! But then, why would my uncle lie?

My thoughts raced. Perhaps Aldo was missing because he was back in time! But the note seemed to say that time here, in the present, stood still while someone was away in the time machine. Yet time hadn't stood still. People noticed Aldo had gone, and they missed him terribly!

I knew I faced a big decision: do I walk away or take a ride? My heart pounded. I'd make so many people happy if I used the time machine to find Aldo! But how far back in time had he gone? Where would I end up? I might find myself in a time when dinosaurs were alive!

Perhaps I had explorer's blood, like my uncle, because with shaky knees, I clambered onto the machine's seat. It was springy and covered in cracked leather. More questions filled my mind. Which button turns it on? How exactly do I get back? How long does it take to get somewhere?

Then I noticed some labels tied to a few of the buttons and levers. The biggest brass button had a label: "ON".

A label next to an old-fashioned keypad said, "To return to the present, put in the secret number." This made me feel much better. It would be easy to tap in the 8888 from Aldo's note. I could get back home quickly, lock the basement door, and no one would know anything about it.

So, I pressed the "ON" button and waited. Slowly, the engine began to splutter. Cogs under the seat juddered but then clanked to a halt. The engine went dead. No fuel? Was it broken? I pressed the button again. This time the cogs spun, the engine roared, the wings flapped and the machine lifted from the floor in a billow of steam.

The whole machine wobbled precariously. Then I noticed one of the pictures on the basement wall was getting bigger!

It was the star-shaped man. It began to tilt, then spin. A tunnel seemed to open in the wall. The spinning picture shot away, followed by the time machine – with me on board!

The time machine

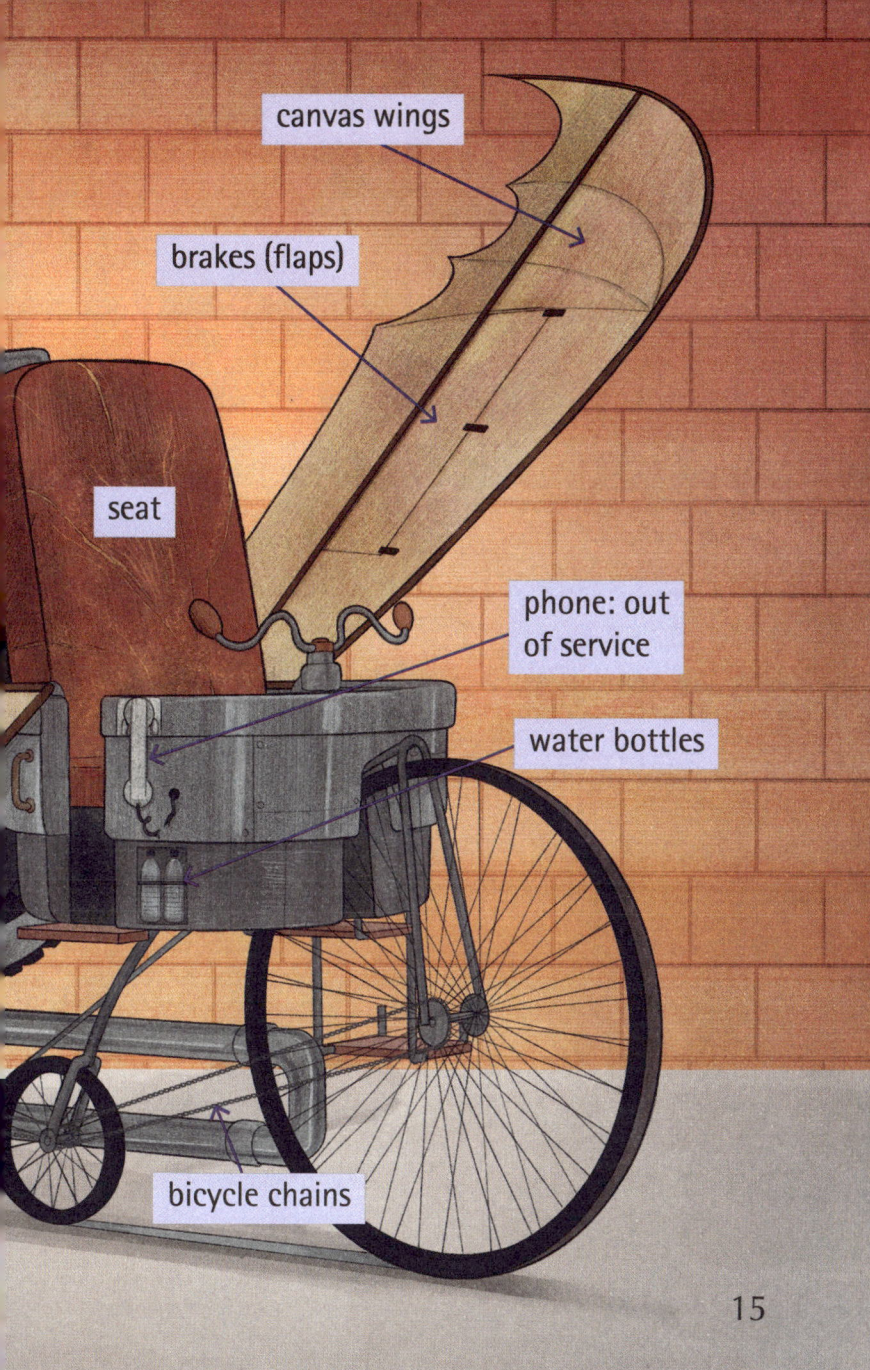

Who was Leonardo da Vinci?

Leonardo da Vinci was born in Italy in 1452. He was fascinated by just about everything and explored lots of subjects, such as maths, anatomy, music and even engineering.

He became a successful artist but was also an inventor.

The painter

Leonardo was trained as an artist but did not finish many paintings.

Today, his painting, the *Mona Lisa*, is one of the best-known works of art in Europe. It's very realistic but no one knows for sure who she was.

The scientist

Leonardo was one of the first artists to study the human body in detail.

The inventor

Leonardo designed and sketched devices like flying machines that didn't exist at the time. No one knows how many of his inventions were ever built or tried out.

Leonardo invented the idea of a parachute.

Chapter 2
Back in time

The time machine lurched left and right, up and down. It was like a rollercoaster! I closed my eyes and held on tight.

I began to feel very sick. Just as I was thinking this whole thing was a terrible idea, the machine began to slow down. After lots of wheezes and clunks, it stopped. There was a warm smell of animals and straw. I opened my eyes in a beam of bright sunshine. I was in a stable. Two chestnut-coloured horses were tied to a pillar. They looked at me for a moment, then carried on munching hay from a trough.

Quickly, I pushed the machine into a corner, so it was hidden behind a broken, wooden cart. A dirty sheet I found was just big enough to cover it. I sprinkled straw across the top. Hopefully, it would be hidden, or I could be stuck here forever!

I crept to the large stable door and peered through a crack. Wow! No dinosaurs, phew! But I could see a huge town square with lots of people milling around, some buying and selling, others just chatting in groups. They were all dressed in weird clothes.

I opened the door just a bit. A massive, elaborate building shone in the sun. It was as big as a cathedral but nothing like anything I'd seen in England. It was shiny and looked brand new!

I jumped as a horse and cart clattered by. The cart was full of oranges, and a boy held the reins. Suddenly, I realised there were no cars or buses, not even bicycles! The people wore long dresses and cloaks, and funny hats. This wasn't England – I was sure of it. So where was I, and *when*?

I listened for clues in what people said as they walked past. But they weren't speaking English. It sounded like Italian – and I didn't know any Italian! But as I listened, I began to pick out some words. Then, the longer I listened ... the more I understood.

Soon, I understood every word! How was that possible?! Was it a special time-travel thing that I could understand the language where I arrived? Wow!

Two bearded men passed close by, chatting. "I hear Michelangelo's working on a huge new statue of David," said one of them. "I wonder how long it'll take him to finish that – if he ever does!"

"Oh, I'm sure he'll finish it," the other man replied. "Michelangelo's reliable – unlike da Vinci!" They both laughed.

"Ah, they say Leonardo is interested in too many things! That's why he rarely finishes a painting!" replied the other man as they walked on.

Suddenly, I knew exactly where I was and when. I remembered a lesson at school about Italian art. Michelangelo and Leonardo da Vinci were artists from at least 500 years ago! They worked in Florence, in a time called the Renaissance. So, I'd travelled back to then! Incredible!

Then I remembered the writing on Aldo's wall – *Leonardo da Vinci*. And of course, there was the painting – the *Mona Lisa* – I was sure it was by Leonardo da Vinci! So did Uncle Aldo have something to do with Leonardo? Perhaps if I found Leonardo, I'd find some clues, or even Uncle Aldo himself!

But how could I go into the street dressed in jeans and a purple jumper?! I'd stand out a mile! I searched the stable. An old smock was hanging on a nail – a cap, too.

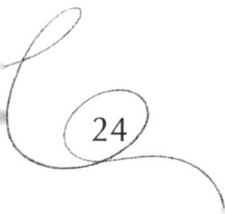

They looked like the clothes the boy on the horse and cart was wearing. *I'll borrow these*, I thought. *Surely they won't be missed.* I put them on over the top of my clothes, and set off.

I spotted a young boy, about my age, carrying a basket.

"Excuse me – " I started to say, then stopped. He probably wouldn't understand English, would he? But I carried on. "I'm looking for Leonardo da Vinci." And something very strange happened. I spoke in English, but Italian came out of my mouth! Time travel let me speak Italian as well as understand it! Amazing!

"His workshop's here." The boy drew a simple map with the point of his shoe in the dusty ground. "But if you're hoping to be an apprentice, I wouldn't turn up smelling of horse manure!" He laughed and walked on.

I flapped my arms as I set off, hoping it would get rid of the stable smells. I followed the route the boy had shown me.

I turned left and saw a tall, fancy-looking building. Above the door I read:

Just then, the door opened and six boys swarmed out. Some were about my age, others were older.

I tried to look casual, nudging a pebble with my foot.

"Be back in an hour, boys!" yelled a voice from a courtyard I could just see through the door.

The boys wore aprons, smeared with paint. Perhaps they were apprentices. But they were *all* boys. I knew girls were excluded from doing lots of things in the past – often the most interesting! I tried to think of any Renaissance artists who were women. Perhaps there were some, but they weren't well-known. *Typical*, I thought. Nearly all the famous people in history seem to be men!

For now, it looked like I'd have to pretend to be a boy to pass as an apprentice and get into the building. Perhaps I'd find Uncle Aldo inside. I took a deep breath and knocked on the door.

Florence in the time of Leonardo da Vinci

When Leonardo lived and worked in Florence, it was a centre of learning and art. It was a time called the "Renaissance" when art and culture became very popular. Renaissance means "rebirth".

Florence, 1493

Lots of artists went to live in Florence and many young people went there to learn as apprentices.

The artist Michelangelo worked in Renaissance Florence. One of Michelangelo's most famous sculptures is called *David*.

Florence cathedral today – parts of it were still being built in Leonardo's day.

Chapter 3
Leonardo da Vinci

The door flew open and a man with a beard and unfriendly face glared at me. He held an artist's paintbrush.

"Please may I see Leonardo da Vinci about being an apprentice?" I said quietly.

"No spaces left!" boomed the man.

I turned to run away when a kinder voice called out. "Let him in, Tomasso! He might be talented."

The man, Tomasso, ushered me in with a growl.

An older man walked slowly across the sun-filled courtyard towards me. He had dark, twinkling eyes and hair that stuck out from under a soft black hat. His beard was the wildest I'd ever seen.

I tried not to stare. Was this THE Leonardo da Vinci? The greatest artist ever ... the man who painted the *Mona Lisa*?!

"Can you show me your drawing skills?" he asked.

My heart sank. "Err, yes," I said. I could doodle, but that was all!

I followed him up a narrow stone staircase into a cool, stone-walled room. Desks and chairs, and stacks of wooden easels filled the room.

"Leonardo, you're wasting your time," said Tomasso.

Leonardo ... So it *was* Leonardo da Vinci! I hoped they wouldn't notice that I was trembling.

"Here, sketch something!" said Leonardo, looking at me encouragingly.

He held out a feather, not a pencil or pen. My heart sank. It was a quill! I'd seen quills on TV, but I'd never used one. I dipped the end of it into an inkpot, then pressed it down to draw a line. Splat! A shower of dots shot across the paper.

"Oh no! Sorry," I said, and tried again. The quill was scratchy, and I didn't know what to draw. I was OK at cartoony doodles, so I started to draw the big eyes and wild hair of one of my favourite characters.

"Ah!" chuckled Leonardo. "You're left-handed – just like me!"

Tomasso tutted behind my back, and said, "His style is too dated."

Leonardo smiled at me. "We want realism these days – what you see, not what you imagine," he said.

"I can learn," I said. "I'd like to learn ... from you." I definitely didn't want Tomasso as my teacher!

"And indeed you will," said Leonardo. "I can't throw a fellow left-hander out! Now, boy, what's your name?"

"Err ... Mario," I said, feeling bad about lying. But there was no way I'd give my real girl's name.

"Tomasso – show Mario his accommodation." He turned to me. "If you're hungry, you'll find food in the kitchen."

"The dormitory is full," said Tomasso, firmly.

"Hmm. Well, Mario – could you bear to sleep in the storeroom for now? We can get some straw and blankets."

"Oh, that'd be perfect. Thank you!" I said. That was lucky! How could I keep up my "boy" disguise in a dormitory full of male apprentices?

After eating a plateful of crusty bread and crumbly cheese, I was back at my desk with the quill again. There were ten other apprentices of different ages, including some grown men. I thought of Uncle Aldo and peered at each older face.

None of them looked like the photos I'd seen of him. Had he ever been here? I'd have to listen for clues. Perhaps I could ask someone if they knew him. I didn't dare yet, though.

Leonardo started the lesson. "Write today's date at the top of your paper."

I sneaked a look at the boy sitting next to me. He wrote:

VI ·XV ·MDIV

Latin numerals. I'd learnt them at school. The month came first, the day next and the year last. I focused on the year – M was a thousand, D was 500, IV was 4. Wow – I'd travelled back to 1504!

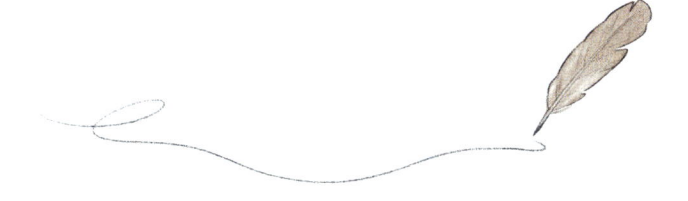

My brain whirled as I tried to concentrate on what Leonardo was saying. He was explaining how to draw lifelike people. Then he pulled up a cloth and there it was – the same image of the star-shaped man that was in Uncle Aldo's basement! Leonardo started to explain how to draw perfectly proportioned people. He talked about measuring different points. He pointed at different places in the picture with a stick. I really couldn't follow what he was saying. I sank into my chair. What if there was a test afterwards!

The star-shaped man made me think about the machine, the bumpy, weird journey, Uncle Aldo's house and Mum. I suddenly felt totally out of place, scared and homesick. I was over 500 years from my own time and pretending to be a boy! What if someone found the time machine? Anyone could try tapping numbers in, get the right one and set off. I'd be trapped here!

I thought about jumping up right then and running back to the stable. More than anything, I wanted a hug from Mum.

But on the other hand, here I was listening to the famous Leonardo da Vinci himself! And if anyone was going to find out what happened to Uncle Aldo, it was me, here, now. There were too many links between Uncle Aldo's basement and Leonardo to ignore. I had to stay.

When I'm stressed, I doodle random things. And I was super-stressed in that room! So I was doodling away when Leonardo shouted, "Mario! Are you listening?"

I gulped.

"Sorry, sir. I was just – "

He walked over to me. "What are these?" he asked. He pointed at my scribbled cartoon helicopters, their weird faces grinning. Trembling, I wondered what sort of punishments 16th-century teachers used on daydreaming students.

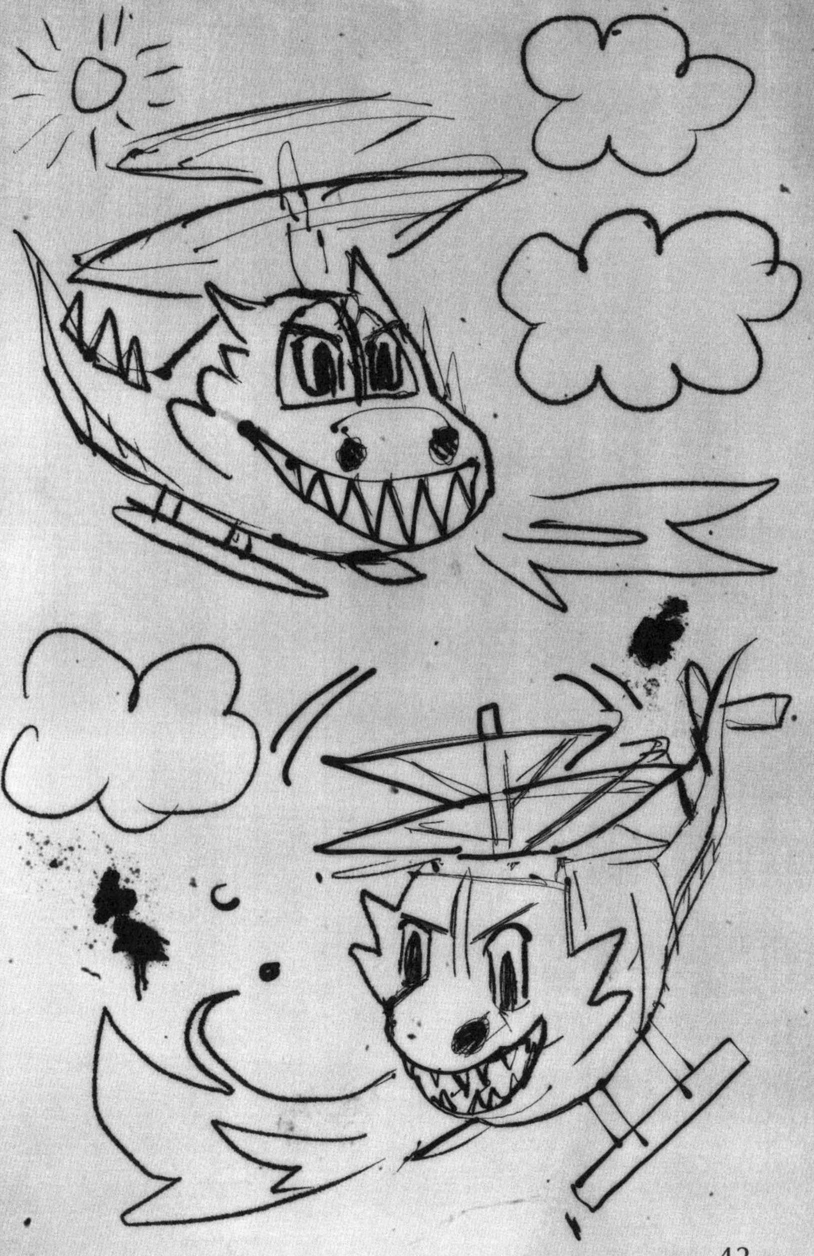

Leonardo, the artist

Leonardo's paintings and drawings were very realistic. Before him, portraits usually showed people stiffly posing, without emotion. Leonardo's people often seem to be deep in their own thoughts.

Without lines

Leonardo was also one of the first to blend paint colours so there were fewer hard lines or borders. This made surfaces, like skin and fabrics, look more realistic.

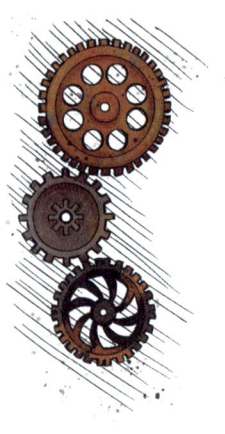

Chapter 4
Good friends

What should I say to Leonardo? Should I explain that my doodles were fantasy-style helicopters ... that their faces and tails were meant to look like a dragon's? Leonardo might know about dragons but helicopters hadn't been invented yet – or so I guessed.

At last, I answered, "Sorry. They're just things from my imagination."

Leonardo told the class to read through their notes, then left the room. I waited, chewing at my nails. Then I remembered Mum would be furious if I came home with chewed nails, so I stopped.

After a few minutes, Leonardo came back and showed me a sketch.

It was so odd! He'd drawn a machine with blades going round at the top. It looked a lot like he was trying to invent a helicopter!

"See – I sketched something similar a while ago! These bits at the top will spin to lift the machine into the sky."

He pointed at the rotors at the top of one of my helicopters. "And you had the same idea. Remarkable!"

I wanted to say, "Great minds think alike," but I thought that would sound a bit cheeky.

He whispered, "I think that, like me, you are more interested in inventions than painting. Perhaps you would like to look at my designs?"

I nodded – of course I would!

Leonardo took me into a room with people painting at easels. He gave me a huge pile of papers from his notebooks.

"Thank you, sir," I said. Some of the pages looked like those on Uncle Aldo's basement walls. Was this a new clue that Uncle Aldo had been here?

"Look at this," said Leonardo, pointing to a sketch of another flying machine.

"Instead of rotors at the top, this one has two wings – one either side. If we build it, I believe it will fly just like a bird."

I definitely didn't think it would fly! I imagined it dropping out of the sky. I'd read a library book called *The Invention of Flight*. Lots of people in history had tried to make planes and failed. Some inventors died when their planes fell to the ground.

I couldn't say what I thought, so I politely said, "That's really interesting, sir."

"Take your time looking at these, Mario," he said. "And please call me Leo."

I thanked him. So now "Leo" was my friend!

For the rest of the day, I looked through his papers. He was way ahead of his time. An amazing inventor! There were sketches of watercraft, even a kind of submarine! There were self-driving carts, and what looked like a parachute. The strange-looking flying machines were amazing.

Most of all, I loved his sketches of mythical creatures. Like me, Leo drew dragons, but his were much better than mine!

I started to think that if Leo was an inventor, then that's probably why Aldo was interested in him. After all, Uncle Aldo had invented a time machine.

I skimmed Leo's notes for the name "Aldo" but it was hard to make out the handwriting. There was only one thing left I could do: ask someone if they knew Uncle Aldo.

Tomasso started working at the same table, grinding and mixing paint. I decided that I'd risk asking him. He seemed to know a lot about who came to the workshop.

Because I felt shy, I kept putting it off. Then Tomasso asked me to pass him a jug of water. I was in the middle of carrying a stack of papers across the room and made the mistake of saying, "Of course – just a minute."

His face went as red as the paint he was stirring, and he yelled, "How dare you, boy! Such insolence. I do not wait even a second for you!"

I didn't dare speak to him again. I definitely wasn't going to ask a question. I felt like giving up and going home.

Later, I overheard Leo chatting with Tomasso about the flying machine. As usual, I listened out for clues about Uncle Aldo. Tomasso started flapping his big arms like a clumsy duck, and said, "Leo, we must try it out. I can build it. Then you can fly it! A few flaps of your arms and you'll be flying like a bird!"

Leo waved me over and explained, "Tomasso is going to build my flying device, then test it by launching me from the top of a tower. At last, I'll fly!"

My blood went cold. I had to stop this, or Leo would plunge to his death! I'd have to be very careful if I tried to explain why it wouldn't work. I couldn't talk about modern planes and jet engines.

Carefully, I just said, "It might be too heavy – maybe you need extra power too? I'm not sure someone's arms are strong enough to keep it in the air."

Tomasso's nostrils flared. "How dare you suggest Leo's arms are weak!"

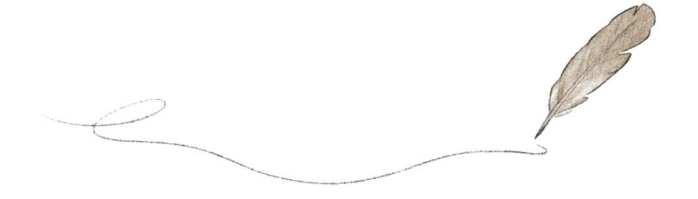

Leo looked at me thoughtfully, then at Tomasso. "Perhaps Mario is right and we shouldn't take the risk – "

Laughing, Tomasso said, "Don't be silly! It's a brilliant design – and I'm a brilliant builder!"

Leo nodded.

Tomasso turned to me. "You, boy, can carry the device up the tower as you think Leo is so weak!"

So I had no choice but to go along with this disaster of a plan. Leo would probably drop to the ground and die, and I would end up in prison for being part of it all. I felt sick.

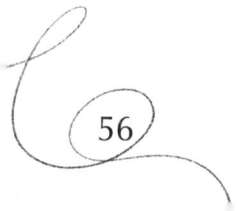

57

Chapter 5
The experiment

That night I twisted and turned on my scratchy straw bed. I thought about sneaking off to the time machine and escaping, but I couldn't leave Leo to die!

In the morning, I sat alone in the workshop. It was the apprentices' day off. Tomasso was building the flying machine in the courtyard. Leo was in his study.

I felt like crying – the whole thing had become such a nightmare, and I hadn't got any more clues about Uncle Aldo.

I decided to explore. There were three easels in the room, each covered in a cloth. I lifted the first two. Both were part-finished portraits of men. Then I lifted the third cloth – wow – those same piercing eyes! It was the *Mona Lisa*! The same picture as on Aldo's wall. It wasn't finished but there it was – the most valuable painting ever. Or at least it would be – in the 21st century! There was something about her half-smile that gave me a sense of hope.

At that moment, two artists came in carrying brushes, and wooden palettes.

"Are these your paintings?" I asked.

"No – they're Leo's," said one of the artists. "He often leaves paintings unfinished. He gets distracted, with all those inventions. We finish them for him."

"What about this one?" I pointed at the *Mona Lisa*.

"Leo won't let us touch that one!" complained the other artist.

Suddenly, I saw an opportunity. "Do any other artists come here and help? A man called Aldo, maybe?"

I held my breath.

The younger artist shrugged, but the older one said, "Aldo? He was Leonardo's friend. They shared an interest in inventing machines."

I tried to stop myself from jumping up and down in excitement.

The younger artist stroked his beard and said, "Ah, yes – Aldo! He had an argument with Tomasso a couple of months ago and left. Hasn't been seen since. No one knows where he went."

I could hardly believe it. Uncle Aldo had been here! But now he'd GONE!

Just then the door swung open and Leo strode in. "Mario, come and see – Tomasso has finished building the flying device. It's beautiful!"

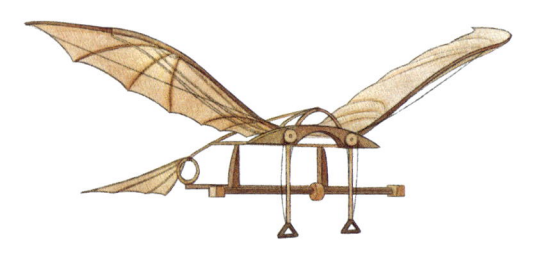

Leo's flying machine stood in the middle of the courtyard – a huge skeleton of wood, its wings stretched out like a bat's. It was amazing! But there was so much wood! It would never lift up without the power of a big engine. It would just drop like a stone.

"Tomorrow, Leo, you fly!" said Tomasso, looking very pleased with himself.

I felt so angry with Tomasso. He was putting Leo's life in danger AND he'd driven Uncle Aldo away!

I could hardly speak. "It's ... err ... it looks amazing." I made an excuse and went inside. I had to speak to Leo alone.

For the rest of the day, I sat looking at Leo's sketches, thinking about Uncle Aldo and where he might have gone. Leo had left the workshop for a meeting, so there was no chance of speaking to him yet.

Bedtime came, and Leo was still out. Tomorrow he would be getting into that stupid machine that wouldn't fly.

All night, I lay awake in a sweat, my heart pounding. Then, just before dawn, Tomasso opened the door to my room. He waved a lamp in my face and gruffly told me to get up.

While most of Florence still slept, Tomasso led me, Leo, and a group of men who carried the flying machine, down the street. I felt numb – it was a living nightmare.

We reached a tower next to the cathedral. There were over 400 steps to climb. To get the machine up the narrow, winding staircase it had to be taken apart. The wings were lifted up outside, using ropes and a pulley.

Halfway up the steps, I looked down at the people in the square. I wanted to shout, begging them to stop the experiment. I nearly screamed, "Aldo – where are you?" But there was no point and Tomasso would probably lock me up.

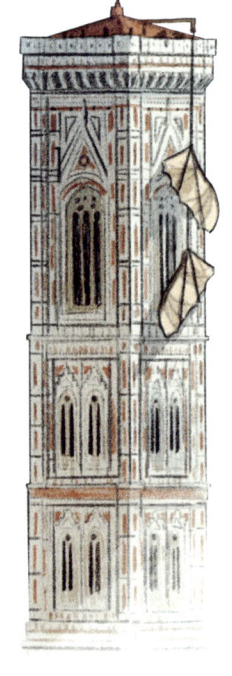

Tomasso and his helpers started to reassemble the machine at the top of the tower.

Tomasso bellowed orders. "Put that there. Screw this tighter. Oil the joints."

Leo stood deep in thought, looking out across the rooftops. I tiptoed over to him, hoping Tomasso wouldn't notice.

"Please don't do this experiment, Leo. I know I'm only an apprentice but I think your machine needs more work. I don't mean to be rude but it's too risky."

Leo looked at me. "I know there's a risk," he said, sadly. "But in Florence people laugh at me because I don't finish things. I don't finish paintings. So I must finish this one thing – my invention."

I turned away, tears in my eyes. What more could I do?

I watched as Tomasso checked the machine, and Leo got ready to climb in.

The men slid a stone battlement aside, then pushed the machine into the gap. It hung precariously over the edge.

Leo strapped himself in.

Leo called to Tomasso, "It's not too breezy, is it?"

In fact, a wind had begun to blow.

Tomasso laughed. "You're not getting scared, are you?"

After a few more adjustments to the machine, Tomasso shouted, "Go!"

I shouted, "Don't do it! Please – " But the wind blew my voice away.

I ran to grab the machine, but Tomasso pushed me aside.

The machine teetered on the edge. I closed my eyes.

Suddenly I heard a voice – thunderous and louder than the wind. "Stop! I demand it!"

The first aeroplane

The first successful aeroplane was called the *Wright Flyer*. It made its first flight in December 1903 – more than 400 years after Leonardo da Vinci drew his flying machines. The *Wright Flyer* was invented by two American brothers, Wilbur and Orville Wright.

Orville Wright

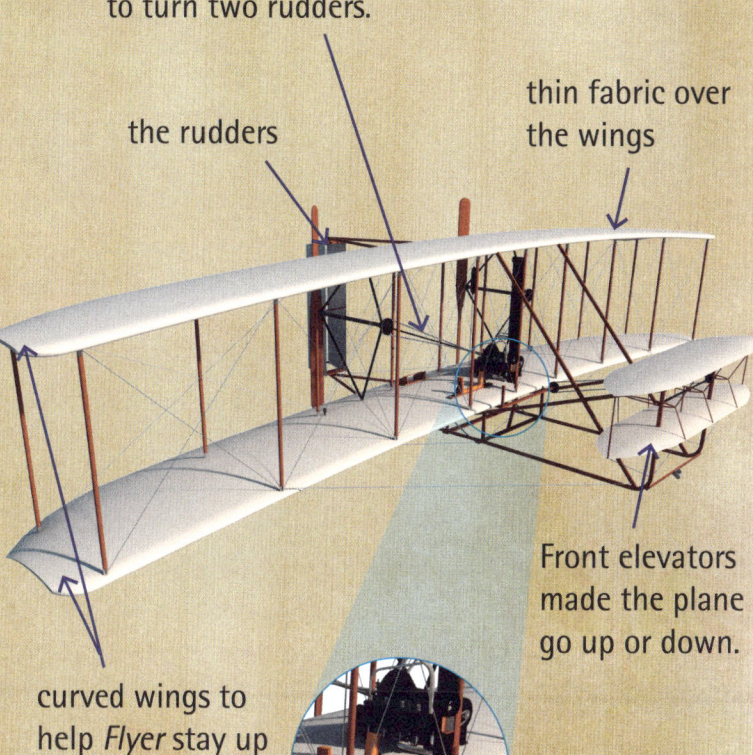

The engine used bicycle chains to turn two rudders.

the rudders

thin fabric over the wings

Front elevators made the plane go up or down.

curved wings to help *Flyer* stay up

The pilot used a stick to move the front elevators.

69

Chapter 6
Lost and found

Everyone looked round. A tall man held a walking stick in the air. "I said, stop!" he yelled.

Tomasso shouted. "Go away!"

"I will *not*! Why choose a tower, Tomasso? Don't you care for Leo's life?"

Leo unstrapped himself from the machine, staggering in the wind. "Aldo! My dear friend!" he cried. "Where have you been all these weeks?"

The machine was dragged from the edge and the experiment was postponed.

That afternoon, voices boomed from Leo's study. Tomasso and Aldo yelled; Leo tried to calm them.

Aldo? It had to be my Great Uncle Aldo - surely! He had a pointy chin and hazel eyes, just like Mum and me. Eventually, the three men came out. Aldo and I exchanged glances.

Aldo turned to Leo, saying, "You have a new apprentice?"

"Yes," said Leo. "This is Mario. An inventor like me! Mario, we've decided to test the flying machine on a hill above a river instead of the tower. So if it fails, there will be a splash – not an – er – "

"Splat," finished off Aldo. "Well done, Mario, for trying to stop the tower launch."

I didn't get to see Aldo again until the next morning. We stood with Leo on a hillside. The flying machine was pointing towards the river below.

Aldo insisted Tomasso flew it this time, so Tomasso climbed in.

The machine slid off the slope. It glided for a few seconds ... then dropped. Splash!

Tomasso clambered out of the river, wet, muddy and very cross.

As Leo went to Tomasso, I whispered to Aldo, "May I ask? Are you from Coventry?"

He nodded. "I am! You seem familiar – ?"

"I'm your great-niece! My name is Maria and I'm ten."

"Oh! How marvellous! When I saw you, I thought, now there's a time traveller from the future!"

"How did you know?" I asked.

He pointed at my ankle – my jeans were showing.

"Denim hasn't been invented yet!" chuckled Aldo.

I grinned. I was SO happy.

Later that evening, Aldo explained how he'd sent the machine back because he loved living in the Renaissance. I explained how everyone was upset because he was missing.

Uncle Aldo felt bad. "I thought time would stand still while I was away!" he said. "I thought no one would notice I was gone!"

"Perhaps time does stand still for a bit, but not for years," I said.

"I'm so fascinated by the Renaissance, Maria. I really want to stay." He grasped my hand. "But you must go back to your mum."

"I will – but I understand why you want to stay."

Uncle Aldo smiled. "I'm so pleased you found the machine and met Leonardo."

Uncle Aldo insisted we went to check the time machine straight away. As we walked to the stable, he said, "I'm going to Germany tomorrow. A man is inventing the first watch! I want to find out how he does it!" Then he asked me about my life, Mum, and school.

In the stable, the machine was just as I'd left it! Uncle Aldo checked the engine and cogs.

"It'll get you home safely," said my great-uncle. "It's yours now. Use it wisely!"

That evening, we hugged each other goodbye. We both cried a bit but promised to meet again one day.

I couldn't leave until I'd said goodbye to Leo. So first thing in the morning, I knocked on his door. I felt sad to leave. But I needed to get back to Mum.

"I'm so sorry ... but my mum needs me," I explained. "Thank you so, so much for my time as an apprentice."

Leo smiled. "Mothers are important – but don't forget to work on your inventions, too!"

I promised I wouldn't forget.

Just as I was leaving, he gave me one of his drawings of a dragon to keep.

"Thank you," I said. "Thank you for everything!"

I ran to the stable. I was going home!

I pulled off the cover and jumped on board.

I didn't feel afraid this time. I pressed the "ON" button and keyed in 8888. The machine began to lift ... The last thing I saw of Renaissance Florence was a snorting horse.

My return journey wasn't as rocky, but I held on tight. Eventually, I landed in Uncle Aldo's basement with a bump.

I sprinted upstairs to Mum. She was still piling Aldo's clothes into bags for charity. No time had passed! She was surprised when I hugged her tightly.

"Mum," I said, "I don't think we need to sell the house. I found this! It might be worth a lot .... It looks like it's by a famous artist!"

I held the dragon drawing out for Mum to see.

She gasped when she saw the signature: *Leonardo da Vinci.*

After that, things happened in a whirl. We took the picture to an expert, who told us it was worth thousands of pounds. We sold it to a museum, and Mum used the money to pay all the bills.

We decided not to sell Uncle Aldo's house, but to move into it ourselves. It was nice to think that if Uncle Aldo ever came back, he'd find us there

Mum told me that the basement was mine – for music, art, anything at all!

One day, I'll explain everything to Mum and tell her Uncle Aldo was okay. But it will be super-hard for her to believe I'd actually time travelled!

But right now, I want to focus on drawing and inventing.

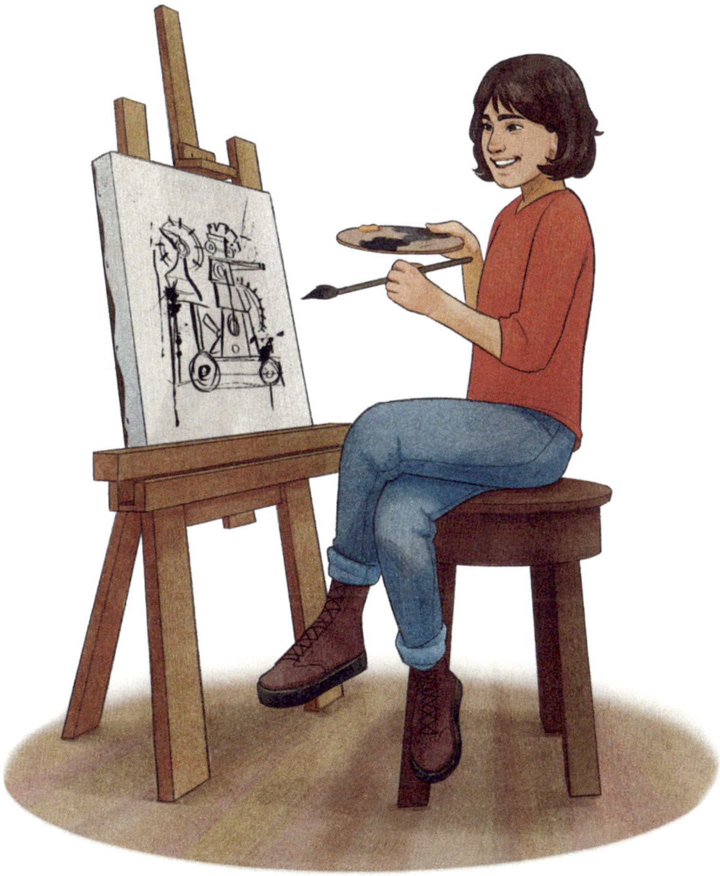

What Leonardo da Vinci left us

Here are just a few of the things.

Art

- seven paintings done with other artists
- lots of unfinished paintings (many of which are still to be found!)
- 13 paintings by himself

Sketches and notes

- 4,000 sketches
- 7,000 notebook pages

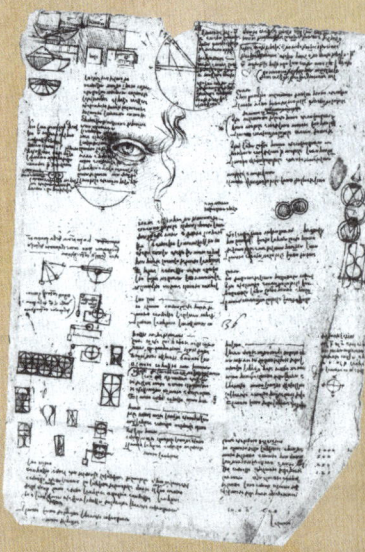

Engineering and technology designs

- helicopter
- parachute
- diving suit
- armoured vehicle
- submarines and boats

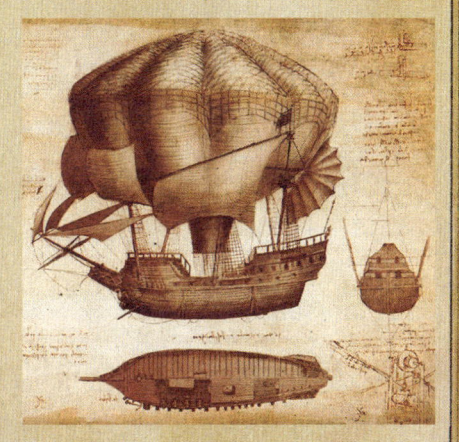

Studies in biology

- human proportions
- work on animals and insects

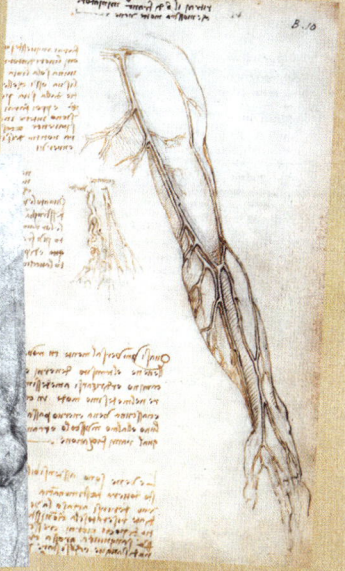

Renaissance women

Women were not encouraged to be artists in Renaissance Italy.

But some women were determined to become skilled painters and sculptors. They are less talked about than male artists, even today. Yet they created many great works

Properzia de' Rossi (1490-1530)

De' Rossi taught herself to carve material like marble. She was the first known female professional sculptor in Europe.

Plautilla Nelli (1524-1588)

Much of this artist's work has been lost or destroyed. She lived in a convent in Florence.

Marietta Robusti (1550-1590)

Robusti trained in the workshop of her father, Jacopo Tintoretto, a well-known artist.

About the author

What made you want to write this story?

Ever since I started watching Dr Who as a child, I've thought that it would be very exciting to time travel. Writing a story about time travel seemed a good way of almost experiencing it for myself!

Liz Miles

How did you come up with the idea for this book?

I've always been keen on art, even though I'm not very good at it myself. So, the idea of meeting an important artist like Leonardo da Vinci through time travel sprang into my mind.

What do you think is the best thing Leonardo da Vinci left behind?

It's hard to say because all his drawings, paintings and inventions are wonderful. If I had to choose one, I'd choose his painting of the Mona Lisa. The woman in the portrait is so alive, and her eyes seem to follow you around.

Why did you choose Coventry for Aldo's home?

Because my great grandfather lived in Coventry, and – guess what? – he was a watchmaker too, just like Aldo!

Why did you set the story in Renaissance Florence?

I've been lucky to visit Florence by train with a backpack and tent. In the galleries and on the streets, I felt a buzz of energy. I wondered what the energy would have been like in the Renaissance when people were trying out all kinds of new ideas. I could easily imagine walking around the streets of Florence during the Renaissance.

What do you hope readers will get from the book?

I hope readers will feel inspired by how Leonardo da Vinci didn't stick to doing just one thing all his life. He explored lots of different subjects, like maths, art and science. This led him to develop some amazing ideas of his own.

If you could time travel, where and when would you like to go and why?

First of all, I would like to go far, far back in time, before people even lived on Earth! I'd like to land on a hilltop where I could look down at dinosaurs below – from a safe distance. I'd like to see what the dinosaurs were really like.

I'd also like to go and meet an artist called Frida Kahlo who lived in Mexico. She painted portraits of herself and was inspired by nature. I've never been to Mexico, and it would be a good way of getting used to time travel. I'd only have to travel back about 70 years to meet her.

About the illustrator

What made you want to be an illustrator?

For most of my childhood, I didn't actually know what I wanted to be when I grew up. I changed my mind often when grown-ups asked me. Usually I told them I wanted to be a doctor or a vet.

Alisha Monnin

When I got closer to leaving home for college, I had an art teacher who thought I had some real talent in drawing. She was the first person to encourage me to pursue art as a career. I'm very grateful to her for believing in me, and now I get to draw all day for work!

What did you like best about illustrating this book?

I loved designing the time machine and drawing the architecture of Florence. I visited Florence for the first time last year. I was excited to use the photos I had taken and imagine what the city might have looked like hundreds of years before.

What was the most difficult thing about illustrating this book?

The most difficult part was also the Florentine architecture! As fun as it was to draw, it took me a long time to get all of the details. Giotto's Bell Tower especially was very detailed and I spent quite a few hours getting the top of the tower drawn just right.

Do you have a favourite character in this book?

My favourite character is Maria. I thought she was very brave to get on her uncle's time machine to go looking for him! She also has a wonderful mind and a drive to create that I admire.

Did you enjoy designing the time machine?

Yes, it was so much fun to design. I sketched a few different versions before settling on the one that ended up in the book. I especially enjoyed drawing all of the exhaust pipes!

What time period would you travel to if you had a time machine?

I would love to go back in time to either ancient Greece or ancient Egypt. Both civilizations constructed buildings that were astounding for their time. Mostly I want to see how they built everything without modern technology.

Book chat

If you had to give the book a new title, what would you choose?

Did any of the characters change from the start of the book to the end?

Would you have tried out the time machine if you'd found it?

Do you have a favourite part of the story? Why do you like that part?

Do you think this book would make a good film? Why or why not?

If you could borrow the time machine, where and when would you like to go and why?

If you could meet Leonardo da Vinci, what would you ask him?

Why do you think Uncle Aldo stayed back in time?

What do you think Maria should do next with the time machine?

Book challenge:

Design your own time-travel machine.

Collins BIG CAT

Published by Collins
An imprint of HarperCollins*Publishers*

The News Building
1 London Bridge Street
London SE1 9GF
UK

Macken House
39/40 Mayor Street Upper
Dublin 1
D01 C9W8
Ireland

© HarperCollins*Publishers* Limited 2024

10 9 8 7 6 5 4 3 2 1

ISBN 978-0-00-868111-1

All rights reserved. No part of this publication may be reproduced, stored in a retrieval system, or transmitted in any form by any means, electronic, mechanical, photocopying, recording or otherwise, without the prior written permission of the Publisher or a licence permitting restricted copying in the United Kingdom issued by the Copyright Licensing Agency Ltd, 5th Floor, Shackleton House, 4 Battle Bridge Lane, London SE1 2HX.

British Library Cataloguing-in-Publication Data
A catalogue record for this publication is available from the British Library.

Download the teaching notes and word cards to accompany this book at:
http://littlewandle.org.uk/signupfluency/

Get the latest Collins Big Cat news at
collins.co.uk/collinsbigcat

Author: Liz Miles
Illustrator: Alisha Monnin (Astound Illustration Agency)
Publisher: Laura White
Product manager and commissioning editor: Caroline Green
Series editor: Charlotte Raby
Development editor: Catherine Baker
Project manager: Emily Hooton
Copyeditor: Sally Byford
Proofreader: Catherine Dakin
Cover designer: Sarah Finan
Typesetter: 2Hoots Publishing Services Ltd
Production controller: Katharine Willard

Printed in the UK.

MIX
Paper | Supporting responsible forestry
FSC
www.fsc.org
FSC™ C007454

This book is produced from independently certified FSC™ paper to ensure responsible forest management.

For more information visit: www.harpercollins.co.uk/green

Made with responsibly sourced paper and vegetable ink

Scan to see how we are reducing our environmental impact.

Acknowledgements
The publishers gratefully acknowledge the permission granted to reproduce the copyright material in this book. Every effort has been made to trace copyright holders and to obtain their permission for the use of copyright material. The publishers will gladly receive any information enabling them to rectify any error or omission at the first opportunity.

p16t Dennis Hallinan/Alamy, p16b IanDagnall Computing/Alamy, p17t Jievani/Shutterstock, p17b Science history images/Alamy, p30 Pictures Now/Alamy, p31t DiVNA/Shutterstock, p31b ChiccoDodiFC/Shutterstock, p44 The Print Collector/Alamy, p45 IanDagnall Computing/Alamy, p68 NG Images/Alamy, p69 background Emmanuel Vidal/Shutterstock, p82t IanDagnall Computing/Alamy, p82bl Keith Corrigan/Alamy, p82br Incamerastock/Alamy, p83t Matthew Corrigan/Alamy, p83bl The Print Collector/Alamy, p83br Album/Alamy, p84 The Picture Art Collection/Alamy, p85t ARTGEN/Alamy, p85bl ARTGEN/Alamy.